The Dominant Wife Rule Book - Chastity Device Edition

"Guidelines for the submissive husband"

By Mistress Jessica
ISBN: 9781500835347
First Edition

This book is for entertainment purposes only

The idea is that with good communication between partners, healthy role playing can be obtained by both parties consenting and agreeing on each role they will play during this time. As with anything respect for both partners is adamant and expected by all involved. Safe words and Safe Gestures should always be employed to ensure that the submissive person has a way regardless of the situation to be able to communicate with the dominant person, these and all ground rules should be set up prior to any role playing of any kind.

You and only you are responsible for your actions.
Have fun, but play safe!
~Mistress Jessica~

Introduction

What it is all about

This book is a sequel or more accurately the next step for the Dominant Wife Rule Book series.

That first book was born out of notes that I had put together while discussing what the basic rules would be in a relationship if one party was to take the lead, in this case specifically if the conventional societal accepted relationship of a Man and a Wife was to be turned on its end. There are many Female led relationships these days it is an exponentially ever increasing number as we progress down the road. There seems to be a strong desire of both genders to switch places, the strong woman yearns to be in control and hold the power, and the weak male longs to be put in his place and submit to the strong woman. Some of you may think this is because the male is thinking this will lead to an increase in the rate of sex between the two, he is usually sorely mistaken. So if you are reading this book out of sequence the first book "The Dominant Wife Rule Book" was about the simple changing of the guard and how the woman of the house takes charge and puts her man in his place. She has taken control of the relationship and is Captain of the ship, this leaves the man being submissive to his wife's needs and wants, she makes the rules and basically he is her bitch to do what she says or be punished.

With that being said…..

The Dominant Wife in Female Led Relationships (FLR) eventually finds herself at the state of having to take away the one thing the submissive male has left that allows him any private joy and pleasure, which would be the control of his cock, or even more importantly the control of his orgasms. Now you may have told him that his cock and balls were yours and you may have even demonstrated this by taking hold of it and smacking it around so he knows who is boss, he may have even cried like the good little submissive he is supposed to be. You probably even made sure that when he was giving you the loving and wonderful attention you deserve with his pathetic excuse for a penis that you made sure he asked permission before being allowed to ejaculate thus ensuring that he understood you were in charge. Eventually though he will find himself alone and it won't take him long before he is touching it and stroking it and just being selfish with it. This just cannot be, after all how many times do you think you are going to be forgiving coming home from a day out and wanting him to perform for you and bring you to that wonderful place where the waves of pleasure flow over your body like the warm ocean on a sunny day. Then looking down at him waiting for him to display his hard and ready member that's only job is to fulfill your every wish and what you see is a limp and tiny little dick.

Oh the excuses will flow he may even cry not understanding why it isn't working; the male species is such a silly creature. The fact is that he just can't leave it alone and finds himself constantly touching it when you are not looking. He won't even be able to give you a reason why when you confront him about it, and there is only one way to make sure that the penis he carries around with him is used only for your personal enjoyment and that it will always be ready when you want it to be ready and that my dear is you are going to have to lock that thing up and keep it under supervision. You would think that all you would have to do is tell him not to play with it unless you tell him so, and I imagine there are few good men out there who can take an instruction like that and live up to it, but alas there are just too many who cannot.

Now some of you may be asking yourself "What do I lock it up with?" well I will get to that in the next chapter my dear.

There is also the possibility that he may have brought the subject up to you and has initiated the conversation about chastity and locking his cock and balls up. You may ask why? Some men find the idea of chastity to be very erotic and just the thought of being restrained gets them excited. When you add the fact that he would be surrendering himself to the woman he is in love with the erotic submission of this act even further heightens his stimulation.

He may understand and grasp the concepts of more than the physical sensations of pleasure seeing as the power of emotion and the psychological pleasures of his mind as something for more powerful and pleasurable then spilling his seed in his hands which is so fleeting and over so quickly.

The idea of being locked up or more so knowing that the key and the power reside in his woman to make the decision to restrain him from self-pleasuring, to grant him the freedom from the over powering urges of his own masculinity, can be very fulfilling.

It might be that he sees himself as being a chronic masturbator and it may be impacting his love making ability, he may be looking for you to help him overcome this dependency on self-pleasure giving him the stamina when you desire him to please you.

He could simply be submissive and the feeling of being owned and controlled is a secret and overwhelming desire for him, the fact that he is bringing this idea to you is a sign of trust as he opens himself up displaying his vulnerability to you, in hopes you will accept him and control him and nurture this secret side of himself.

It may be that he sees you as a strong woman and as such are deserving of his capitulation and submissiveness, in that case it is more like a gift he is offering to you. He is demonstrating your superiority over him and as such is willing to lose himself to demonstrate to you his acceptance of your leadership over him in both mind and body.

He may even find orgasm denial to be very arousing When it comes right down to it regardless of the reasons, one thing is for certain he will be locked up and controlled, and his one and only aim from that day forward is to seek his pleasure in pleasing and pleasuring you. Your needs will now come first and foremost no longer will you be second to anything and you will be given your due right as the leader in the relationship hence forward.

The Chastity Device

The device itself is designed to prevent sexual intercourse, and in the past it was primarily used upon women, so they could keep their virtues intact, it also protected them against rape as well as from sexual temptation.

These days though their certainly are still many devices for keeping a woman's vagina locked up, so many strides have been made in the area of the Male Chastity device.

More often than not the devices are used in BDSM as well as some Vanilla relationships. As one partner gives control to the other, it is often used to ensure long term fidelity as well as making sure that masturbation doesn't take place. The industry has made leaps and bounds in this area of securely holding your male partner's genitalia safe and sound, especially from himself.

The devices themselves can be made of any number of types of materials mostly you will see plastic and metal, though I have seen wooden ones and leather ones as well. It usually takes the configuration of a ring that goes around the balls and the base of the penis and a cage that surrounds the penis that is then pinned to the ring and locked with a simple pad lock.

It is sometimes the case that numbered tie wraps are used this is often the case when a male is playing on line with someone further away than is conveniently able to be traveled to, like online relationships. They give the number to an online partner who can then verify the device hasn't been removed through a web camera or such by seeing the numbered tie is still in place.

The tie wraps can be useful for emergency situations like when traveling and you don't want to explain why your crotch is setting the metal detector off, boy now that has to be humiliating to whisper in the ear of a big TSA agent that you wife keeps your cock locked up and that is what is setting off the alarm.

You know that guy is getting stripped searched for certain may even have to be getting down on his knees to be able to make his plane, what a funny story that would be to tell his wife when he got home from his business trip.

The devices can range in price from say thirty five dollars up to quite a few hundred dollars depending upon where you purchase them. I have found to start out with you can get a reasonable deal on eBay and Amazon.

Though you are in control of your submissive husband you do want to make sure that he is comfortable in the device that it doesn't chafe him or pinch him and so on. Many of the plastic ones come with a number of different sized rings so you can experiment with which ones works the best for him.

I cannot stress the importance of taking the time to get this right in the beginning; it will save you so much grief down the road.

I have some sissy's in my stable that prefer the plastic and some that swear by the metal ones, the main difference I have seen is how the body is effected by the metal or the plastic touching the skin. They have always told me that a little Vaseline around the area where the ring will reside as well as the top of the head of the penis makes everything fit better and can reduce irritation considerably.

It is important for you to be able to put it on and take it off of your submissive husband but let him learn how to do it first, be there and watch him so you can see what works for him and what doesn't. He is usually the best person to find the best way to put it on your possessions. After he does it a few times then you give it a try, in a matter of no time at all you will both become professionals at locking up your cock and balls.

The main difference between the Metal and the Plastic devices is the rings, the plastic ones usually have a cut out that allows you to kind of slide the balls into it with a wiggle or two, then a small plate with pins goes in through the back completing the ring itself and with the pins sticking out allows the front piece to be put in place, they also usually have spacers you will also have to experiment with until you find the right mix. The metal device is usually a solid ring, I have seen them come in different sizes but unlike the plastic ones you usually only get the one ring so make sure you know which ring size you are buying. We will talk about measuring your possessions a little further on. The metal ring is a little trickier as you have to push one ball through the ring and then the second one through, then you have to push the penis into itself and then under the ring so that the whole package now has the ring around them all.

There is also another metal ringed model that has a hinge and will close around the cock and balls, make sure you have the surgical tubing in place over the hinge else this could cause some unnecessary discomfort to the user.

Like I stressed earlier and will once again, you want to make sure the device is comfortable; the enjoyment of discomfort is something that goes beyond the initial wearing of the device. If you're submissive husband is in constant pain or irritation because of simply having the device on, he is not going to be any fun for you if he is constantly telling you how uncomfortable it is.

The real fun comes later when by your actions and desires do you make him shall we say uncomfortable in it.

When it comes to measuring you should measure his cock when it is soft, take a few measurements during different times of the day, measure from the base of the shaft above the ball sack to the tip. When I refer to soft I do not mean shriveled up as some can be sometimes. Take a half an inch of the length measurement just to make sure he is snug. With regard to the rings, if you are buying one of the CB-something's they usually come with a number of ring sizes so you will have to experiment to see which one is the correct fit for your submissive. The overall idea is that you should be able to slide the tip of your finger between the ring and the skin under the ball sack. If you are looking at the metal devices take some string and measure around the balls and cock and determine the diameter from the circumference, now how many of you are saying right now I don't remember how to do that. Well here it is for those who forgot high school math, if you know the circumference and you want to know the diameter take the circumference number and divide it by Pi or (3.14). Since the Metal ones usually but not always have a solid ring they sell them measured that way. Make sure you get the right size ring else you may have some trouble either pushing your balls through the circle or they may have a tendency to slip out, so do the due diligence, you don't want your balls turning blue because your got the wrong size, once a testicle dies because of lack of blood flow it has to be removed, don't kill your testicles because you are lazy.

Safety / Hygiene

Please keep in mind that putting your submissive husband into full time chastity right out of the gate is probably not going to be a good idea for either of you. Can it and has it been done, I am sure it has, but decisions about locking your partner's sex organs behind a cage of plastic or metal should be taken a bit more serious then tying someone up to the bed so you can have your way with them.

Part of your research should include talking to others who are into Chastity, join some group on FetLife or other BDSM social network and read the posts and ask questions. They have a great deal of experience to offer and would like nothing more than to help a lady put her man's cock and balls into a cage. The device is a toy just like any other toy and you need to learn how to use and keep it clean just like you would a vibrator or butt plug.

Once you decide on the device and get it home, let your submissive husband learn how to put the device on before you slam his cock and balls shut in the cage. Some women enjoy putting the device on them, but others enjoy something a bit more fun. I personally like the fact that my submissive puts the device on himself, just think of what must go through there submissive little minds when they realize they are putting a cage around the one thing they could always count on to bring themselves pleasure, even if everything else was taken away they could always whip out there pathetic little cock and stroke it until they shot there load everywhere. Now they will not be able to do that because of the device that they themselves are securing unto themselves.

As I mentioned the most fun is not in putting the device on, the most fun is taking the little lock and sliding it through the hole and looking at their pitiful faces as you click the lock shut.

I have had grown men shed a tear as they heard that click sound knowing they just lost the one thing they could always count on, that they no longer owned their own orgasms. By all means you should learn how to get it off and on him because sometimes you may have a reluctant submissive and those sometimes end up only getting the device removed while they are tied to the bed, this way you can have your fun with the little cock you now own and when you are done you can be sure to lock it up again this way you know where it is at, and more important where it has or hasn't been.

So have your submissive wear the new device for a few hours or most of the day if he doesn't find it uncomfortable. In the beginning I would recommend no sleeping in the device, since the device's main function is to inhibit erections sleeping in it may be very uncomfortable depending upon which device you have as a man may have a number of erections during the night and what can't push out has a tendency to push inward, it could make for a rude and uncomfortable awakening.

As far as cleaning goes I would by some extra Q-Tips as they sometimes are the only way to get into the nooks and crannies of the device. The metal devices do clean up better in the shower but for good hygiene purposes you should still take the time to inspect the device thoroughly you don't want any bacteria growing in places that could get into your urinary tract so do it right.

The Plastic devices are the ones you really have to be careful of as they have a greater tendency to more fully enclose the cock and can easily build up spots that need to be cleaned more aggressively to ensure that you are playing safe.

How you play with your device with regard to keeping your submissive husband locked up is entirely up to you, there is not one way to do it. In the upcoming chapters I will show you a few different ways of going about it.

Communication

Now I know we took some time in going over things that I could have put a little deeper into the book but those things like safety and hygiene are important to know right off the bat.

Let us take a step back now to that time when the subject came up.

The subject of a chastity device should be brought up by the woman; it usually comes across as a threat at first to the man.

"If I catch you fucking around on me I will lock your cock up so only I can have it"

"All you do is look at porn on the internet and jerk off; I should lock that cock of yours up"

"Maybe if you didn't play with it all the time you cock could get hard when it is time to make love"

I am sure many of you have had similar experiences, if you are into the more progressive sex scene or have a Non-Vanilla lifestyle then you know that sometimes the male partner can get carried away and get caught up in all the sex and erotica and finds that he pulling on his cock more than he should and this can have severe ramifications in the relationship. These are some of the reasons why the woman needs to take control of the situation.

By take control we are referring to locking his pathetic excuse of a cock up so that he can't play with it anymore unless you give him permission.

So let's get started.

I am going to include the first few rules we spoke of in the first book because they should be ingrained into the Male Submissive as part of the very foundation of the relationship and are worth mentioning again.

Her word is the Law!

This is always the most important rule of the Female led household, and if you notice there is no check marks for this being a current rule in your household because if you don't abide by this rule in and of itself then you are not really living the lifestyle that this book is written for and you should stop right now and figure another way to amuse yourself.

I mean if you are not ready to accept your wife's word as the law, you are not ready to be submissive, because quite simply put the rest of this book is solely dependent upon you accepting this right from the start.

If she tells you that from now on it is your responsibility to take the garbage out of the kitchen and to the garbage can, she is giving you instructions and you will obey her every command. The above statement should be no different than if she told you to get on your knees and suck off the mailman, you would do as you are told and capitulate to her every desire if you can't say no to the garbage then you can't say no to the sucking the mailman either.

You may think this is all a game but in reality it isn't for a relationship to be successful there has to be some rules and like I said above this is the most important and non-negotiable rule.

Are you truly ready to accept what your wife says as the law, can you accept that and give up control over your own life and give that power to her? I know that you can, after all you already probably take the garbage out so what would it be to do the other things for her I mean you want her to be happy, you want to serve her, you want her to be pleased with your performance don't you. You Love this woman, she is everything and as such you should be willing to do anything for her to make her life easier and more satisfying. You will even give up your own pleasure for her pleasure that could mean not watching football on TV on Sunday but instead go shopping with her or to some chick flick movie if that is what she desires.

No Arguing!

Here is another rule that is not open for negotiations; the submissive husband is not allowed to argue with the Dominant Wife, for any reason what so ever. It is not good form to allow this and any infraction of this needs to be dealt with plain and simply with punishment, specifically I insist that it must be a beating of some type. Even little arguments need to be dealt with severely. The submissive husband must understand that by giving up his power and control he must capitulate to the Dominant Wife in all things that she decides regardless if he agrees with them or not. The fact that the submissive husband talks back or raise his voice means he has not given up his control and will need to be punished for this, I prefer to spank his ass with his own belt for this type of misbehavior.

<u>Listen!</u>
It is so important for your submissive husband to listen to you when you want to talk, and I mean eye contact, engaged the whole works. You want him to give you his full attention, regardless of what it is you are talking about. If you want to speak with him about the butterfly you saw on your way to work he needs to be all ears.

If you find him lacking in this nothing says pay attention than a few goods smacks to your submissive husband's ass while he is lying over the arm of the couch with his pants around his ankles.

No Lying!

I would think this one would be obvious but sometimes it is not, he needs to be completely honest with you in all things. And I mean all things.

If he did something wrong he needs to accept that and tell you about it so that he can have his punishment and feel better for not keeping anything from you.

In the beginning of this transition the submissive husband should be given the opportunity to express all of his secret and most desirable fantasies no matter how dark or how outrageous. It is important to for him to be upfront and regardless of what they are; after all they are just fantasies you should not as the Dominant Wife be upset with him for having them. If he wants to dress up in stockings and a house dress, be accepting of it just as much as if he wants you to take a lover and fluff his cock for him before this lover fucks you. You must accept them as what they are, which is fantasies, it will be up to you as the Dominant Wife to decide if any or all of them should come true.

<u>You will thank your Wife for the discipline and punishments you receive.</u>

You are probably thinking why, what difference does it make. It makes all the difference, the submissive husband must understand that you are doing this for his own good, that if is able to perform his chores and abide the rules you will not have to punish him.

Of course it also makes it a little more humiliating for him to have to do this and that is the part that I have always enjoyed personally.

It is important that your submissive husband accept his role as such, and you being the leader of the relationship you should require his obedience in all things. At the same time though you are going to want to feel the humiliation and the shame of certain things to have him experience by thought and action the fact that you are superior to him and that his acceptance of this is mandatory.

When you decided to put him into Chastity, it is far better for you to have him ask you to put him into chastity. He has already given himself over to you but he must admit to himself that he cannot and should not be in charge of his sex. This is true if he is a sissy or just submissive, he needs to recognize that he doesn't have the self-control required to be allowed access to the one thing that gives him pleasure, that he will openly abuse the privilege of having access to his genitals and since they no longer belong to him he will need to ask or better yet have him beg you to lock them up.

Now obviously people are into different things so the way you introduce chastity to your own personal situation can happen in a number of different ways and you should do so in a way that fits and works well in your personal situation. It all comes down to the fact that your submissive must voluntarily agree to be put into chastity, I mean if he truly loves you then it should not be an issue but he will still have to agree to it.

Once you have agreement then don't waste time and begin to use chastity in a way that makes you happy.

Chastity Device of Her Choosing
( ) Yes
( ) He is not ready for this rule at this time
( ) No

She rules the roost and as such even after getting your input on which device it is that you feel would be good for you, it is solely up to her which device it is she will get.

If she chooses to get one with the spikes that add a little more pain or maybe that really fancy electric one that can be used to give pleasure or pain by electric shocks with the remote control.

It is all up to her.

It shouldn't matter the type of device that is purchased your only job is to please her, and if you are doing a good job at that then maybe she will not need to lock your cock and balls up after all.

Of course if she does, that just means she wants you to work harder to earn the right to have an orgasm, and that they are not free for you anymore.

Note:
Most people end up using the Goldilocks approach. This one is too tight, this one is too uncomfortable, but eventually you will find one that is just right.

She does not require a reason to lock you up
( ) Yes
( ) He is not ready for this rule at this time
( ) No

The simple fact that she wants to know your cock is locked up and that the key she has is the only way to free your cock and balls should be all that is needed or required to put the device on you.

Maybe she doesn't trust you when she is out with the girls, or maybe she doesn't trust you when she is out on a date with a real man.

Maybe it is that time of the month and she doesn't feel like fooling around and doesn't want you to have any fun either. She could have found that weird porn on your computer; you know where the guys dress up as girls.

She could have flipped a coin and you lost.

She is always in control and the more that she is pleased the less pain and discomfort you will be in.

You may not attempt to remove or circumvent the device
( ) Yes
( ) He is not ready for this rule at this time
( ) No

By succumbing to agree to wear the device any attempts to remove the device or to achieve pleasure while wearing the device will be seen as a serious infraction that will result in one or all of the following.

- Longer term wearing the device or being restricted from any physical pleasure

- A new more secure device being purchased

- Spanking with device of her choosing for as many as She feels will fit the deed.

It is very poor form for a submissive to think they have the right to get around wearing the device; it shouldn't matter if she has stopped giving your pleasure for extended periods of time, and you gave that right up when you gave yourself to her. It is your job and responsibility to make sure she is pleasured, only then when she is fully satisfied by whatever means she believes you to be good at whether that is your tongue or the use of a toy or your finger. Only then will she even think of you, and it might simply be to remind you to finish the washing or to clean the kitchen and you will do a good job of that because you do it for her.
Note:

If your boy and I use that term loosely since he is allowing you to lock his cock up has serious problems and you just can't seem to get him to stop wiggling his way out of his device they do make things that can help prevent that, that is depending upon which device you are using. Of course a good paddling usually works well too.

Pleasing only her!
( ) Yes
( ) He is not ready for this rule at this time
( ) No

This is usually the hardest thing the husband in chastity has to learn to accept.

It should be enforced early on and regularly.

Start this when it is time for bed and instruct him to please you either with a toy or with his tongue.

When you are satisfied and have achieved the amount of pleasure you desire, simply roll over and say goodnight. This may be hard at first as you may feel that you should reciprocate but you have to be strong and he has to learn that it is about you and not about him. He might beg or even expect it but you have to be strong and tell him no, if he is to bothersome do not hesitate to go and get the hairbrush and give him a good spanking for being so annoying.

He has to learn that orgasms are something that you and only you can give and they will be few and far between.

Keeping him in this anxious and aroused state will make him more pliable to your wants and desires.

Be Strong about this one!

You will be Clean and Milked
( ) Yes
( ) He is not ready for this rule at this time
( ) No

It is important seeing as you are her property that you are kept up, so make sure you are keeping yourself and the device clean. This includes informing her of any irritations or discomfort so that the device can be adjusted to fit more properly if necessary.

She as your owner will need to learn to milk you so that you don't get built up to badly which could have ill effects. That and it will also be somewhat humiliating to undergo the process of being milked.

They do have devices to help with this but you can use your finger as well, by stimulating his prostate gland through inserting your finger into his rectum you can actually make him relieve his built up balls without achieving an orgasm.

Do some research online to decide the method you want to go about doing this.

You get him up on all fours and go to work, make sure you put a cup or a plate beneath the device, you will know when it is working as his cock will start to drip pre-cum.

When all is said and done it is always good to have him lick it up as one more humiliating thing for him to accept under your leadership.

Some women like to train their men to cum through penetration not an easy thing to do but if you spend the time and find the right strap on, you can make him orgasm through anal sex. Just think of how much masculinity he will lose when that happens.   If you can achieve this then his days of manly orgasms may have just come to an end.

Talking and enjoying the suffering
( ) Yes
( ) He is not ready for this rule at this time
( ) No

You should inform your wife of your experiences, tell her how it feels when you cock has an erection or attempts to have an erection. Explain what got you excited. Tell her how it feels to have to sit down to pee and how when you touch the lock and see Her cock instead of His cock.

When asked tell her your favorite time when you still had control of your cock. Be assured that will never happen again. She truly enjoys knowing things she can do later to make you suffer by getting you excited only to leave you hanging.

Thank her each and every time she locks you up, once you hear the click of the lock you should thank her for taking control of what is now HER cock.

Maybe if he is lucky you can tell him about the really big cock you played with while you were out with the girls and he was home locked up doing chores around the house.

Exposure to Stimulation
( ) Yes
( ) He is not ready for this rule at this time
( ) No

Your owner has the right to expose you to stimulation in any way she deems fit. This could be by pornography or by physical contact. She can touch and tease you until your cock is straining against the device but no true pleasure will be achieved by you only frustration.

This will give her great amusement knowing that there will be no relief unless she says so, and there should never be any expectations of that.

You should take pride and enjoyment in the fact that she is giving you attention, that she is playing with you at all. Make sure you show your appreciation by thanking her every chance you get that she locked your genitals up and have taken control of them.

She always has the right to extend your term of chastity or push out the times when you will be allowed to orgasm.

No Secrets
( ) Yes
( ) He is not ready for this rule at this time
( ) No

As your owner she will wear the key to your device from a
chain or a bracelet so that it will always be close to her. She
will not publically divulge what the key is for, but she will not
lie about it either. So if someone asks about the key she will
tell them truthfully that is for her husband's chastity device.
This can be a hard one but it is so erotic at the same time.
Imagine her coming home from lunch with your mother and
her having to tell you that your mom asked about the key
around my neck. Now she could have told her it was the key
to your heart, but no she told her the truth that it was for your
chastity device. Then the phone rings and guess who it's your
mom.

Or maybe

She stops by the office and your secretary sees the key around
your wife's neck and says "that's cute what is it for?" your
wife just smiles and says that she keeps your cock locked up
and that this is the key. Later that day your secretary is being
much more flirty with you and your cock is straining against
the cage and then she whispers into your ear. "Your wife told
me about your cock cage and how uncomfortable it gets when
it gets hard"
Yup even an evening of poker with the boys at your house
could lead you into dangerous waters as one of your friends
while in the kitchen asks about the key and after finding out
you find him fucking your wife in the bedroom simply
because he knows you have a month left on your chastity
sentence and your wife needed to feel some real cock.
Yup could be interesting indeed.

Clean Shaven
( ) Yes
( ) He is not ready for this rule at this time
( ) No

The crotch area and any other area she sees fit, will remain clean shaven at all times so as to ensure a greater viewing of the device while in place as well as to further demonstrate the submissive continued existence as being not much of a real man. This will also reduce any pinching by the device and prevent even more whining about how uncomfortable it is. Further humiliation may be gained by insisting that panties be worn at all times to further signify his lower standing in the relationship. I would recommend crotch less panties so the device can easily be fed through the panties for the world to see.

This will also be a wonderful way to display your submissive for your girlfriends and lovers. Nothing truly says humiliation like friends and lovers looking at your locked up cock and balls while wearing crotch less panties.

No Touching HER penis
( ) Yes
( ) He is not ready for this rule at this time
( ) No

You will no longer be allowed to touch HER penis and during those times it is out of the chastity device you will either be secured while any touching goes on or you will be instructed under penalty of severe punishment not to touch said penis under any condition.

Obviously there could be doctor visits and such and you don't want to have to explain to someone not in the know why there is a device attached to your husband's genitals. This is not the same for going to the gym or some other social interaction where you may need to undress in front of other men, they should know the type of man you really are so the device will not be removed for those circumstances.

Seeing as it is her penis she may want to play with it, this could be in a pleasurable way or in a painful way that is entirely up to her, so cross your fingers and hope she didn't have a bad day at work and is planning on passing her anger on to you through HER cock and balls by a good beating.

When orgasm does occur
( ) Yes
( ) He is not ready for this rule at this time
( ) No

During those times when orgasm does occur by choice or by accident, you will be required to ingest any cum that comes out of HER penis. This would be on whatever the cum falls upon, so if you cum in your panties then you need to lick it off the panties, if you cum on your hand then fingers into the mouth, if by some amazing reason you find yourself actually having sex with your wife and you cum in her pussy you need to get down there and lick it all back up. If you cum on the carpet or the table don't matter lick it up.

Note:
This rule could also apply to all cum whether it is his or not.

The Coin Toss
( ) Yes
( ) He is not ready for this rule at this time
( ) No

Well if you have had him in chastity for any length of time he is probably itching for ways that he can please you enough where you will let him out of the device or give him some release.

An easy way to start or at least giving him a chance to win an orgasm is the coin toss.

How you get to the reward of the coin toss is up to you, a certain number of orgasms or maybe just a reward chance for doing a good job cleaning up the kitchen.

Pretty simple you flip the coin and he calls it in the air.
If he wins you can either give him a certain amount of time to pleasure himself nothing to extravagant say like five minutes or three minutes?

Of course if he loses he gets nothing and has to impress you again somehow to get another chance to flip the coin.

Ok so now you have probably experimented a little with the device, you have locked him up and he may or may not have had a positive change or reaction to realizing he truly was no longer in charge of his genitals.

Where do you go from here?

A lot depends upon your submissive. Does he find himself more willing to accept his role of being in chastity or is he a rebellious one about it.

Some men will become more attentive and quickly will fall into line realizing that they only have one job that could result in their desire for an orgasm and that is pleasing their woman, and these men will do almost anything. In fact the more that you keep them locked up the more they become only interested in pleasing you. Now there are those that get upset and sometimes angry about always fighting back begging to be let out, trying to sneak out of the device and such, these are the trouble makers and sometimes what begins somewhat as a trust experiment quickly becomes more trouble than its worth. Not everyone is fit for chastity, but for those trouble makers that you still want to put in their place you may have to up your game with some more elaborate chastity devices to better ensure their compliance with your wishes.

I like my men voluntarily on their knees before and I am not into a power struggle you either give me your cock and balls or you don't. Of course I have submissive's waiting in line to join my stable of boys so I don't have to put up with any crap.

So where are we now….

He will not initiate sex anymore
( ) Yes
( ) He is not ready for this rule at this time
( ) No

With the wife in control and the man with HER cock locked up in chastity things around the house will change greatly after that.

Since he has given over his cock and balls to her and they are now HER cock and balls he has nothing to offer her and as such should never ask for sex or any sexual favors.

To do something of the sort is an act that deserves and requires punishment.

If you don't have one go out and get a cane rod, something thin that you could whip his ass good with, now be careful with the cane rods as they can break the skin always start of slowly and build up until you have achieved the amount of welts on his ass that you feel is enough.

Remember if you have broken him correctly he will not try and initiate sex with you, so you can't think of him as a real man anymore and wait for him to make that first move. If you want to have sex you do it, and if it takes other forms such as him licking you till you orgasm and nothing for him then so be it. Maybe sex will now be about penetrating him, or maybe it won't involve him at all anymore it is all up to you.

He will learn better ways to bring you to orgasm with his tongue.

( ) Yes
( ) He is not ready for this rule at this time
( ) No

Since you won't be using his cock any more on a regular basis the only real sex organ he has left at his disposal is his tongue. He should be given ample time to research better and appropriate ways to use this last vestige of pleasure for the sole purpose of bringing you to orgasm.

You should test him on his knowledge he should know and be able to identify the different parts of your vagina and which ones are known to bring pleasure when stimulated and in which order he should do this for you. He should also be able to tell you what your favorite way to be touched in this area is. If he can't do this then there is no chance in hell of him being unlocked for a little play with the penis time anytime soon. Get him started on some women's magazines so he can better understand how to please you, it would do him good to learn more about women in general anyway.

Understanding your toys and how to use them

( ) Yes
( ) He is not ready for this rule at this time
( ) No

Some women are into toys and others are not, if you have one or more toys he will need to become an expert on how you like it used.

Maybe you have a vibrator he should know the proper settings for the speed and intensity and when you like them to be changed.

You may need to sit him down and give him a lesson and let him practice, it will probably take him a little bit as he will more than likely be nervous and if he has been locked up for any length of time by now I am sure he will be uncomfortable in his cage while he learns how you like your toys used.

This would be a good time to reward him if he can truly learn such a daunting task.

Always keep in mind that rewards come in many different sizes, and they most certainly do not have to involve penetration. In fact depending upon how you want him to feel you can give what is known as a ruined orgasm, this is done by you touching him until he is about ready to cum and then letting go so his orgasm is ruined and his cum dribbles out.

You can be very creative in how you allow him to achieve maybe get him a Fleshlight or if you want to humiliate him maybe get him a blowup doll or something like that, totally up to you.

Constant state of arousal
( ) Yes
( ) He is not ready for this rule at this time
( ) No

As the head of the house you should feel free to wear whatever clothing you want to around the house or even nothing at all for that matter.

It is encouraged to wear sexy clothes or just some panties anything that will put your partner in a state of arousal. Feel free to watch porn on the television or computer, put something sexy on just to arouse him and tease him. Do not let him play with you, make sure he realizes that the torment is the game of the day.

Tease him as much as you can gently touch his cage you will enjoy seeing your cock strain against its bonds as it tries to rise to the occasion but is yet unable. Of course he will not enjoy it at all since it will be most uncomfortable for him.

Decisions, Decisions

Obviously you can make up any number of rules and he will follow them like a little lost puppy dog, you have the power after all you have the Key and with that he isn't going to want to do anything that is going to make you upset. Oh he will more so in the beginning since he just hasn't truly accepted his fate, but they usually get better with a little time. As with anything if he was willing to put it on, then he will be willing to pay the price for any mistakes he makes along the way, and that punishment should be something that is both painful and or humiliating.

So you want to let him out and have some fun.

Well that is up to you, you can simply let him but that can lead to him thinking he is gaining his masculinity back, others like to give him the hope of the game of chance.

Dice – you can use these for so many things, you can have him pick a number and if he rolls that number he gets the rest of the day free from being locked up, or maybe he gets to put his cock inside of you. This is totally up to you, if you don't want his pathetic cock inside you and are more happier with the big dildo's you have him use then don't offer him that prize. You own his cock and balls so you can have him go jerk off in the closet, or have him play with himself while you whip his backside, and so on.

They can also be used to decide how long he will be in chastity, depending upon how well things are going and what he can stand you can roll one two or three dice, it would be a very poor time to roll triple sixes, but again that is between you and him.

Cards are also good, each morning you can pick a card and if he can guess it or if it is a certain card that was prearranged then he can come out and play with himself. Get some index cards and write down good things and bad things. They could be gets to have sex with you, or maybe you get to use that strapon up his ass, you could have twists like he can jerk off until he cums but has to use Icy Hot.

The ideas could be endless if you take the time to really give it some thought.

If you have a nice backyard you could take him outside and remove the only key for his device and simply throw it over his head out there into the grass or bushes and tell him he will be given a certain time limit each day to try and find it. Make sure he understands that it is the only key for the device so he will have a sense of urgency. I remember the first time I tried this one, my little chastity slave cried himself to sleep each night.

You can also hide the key in the house and while he is cleaning the house he can look for it.

If you are lucky enough to have a bag of similar keys you could always put the real key into the bag of wrong keys and he can pick one every morning, and see if he was lucky or not.

The Couple

When dealing with a couple who are only interested in each other, there is quite a bit of pleasure that can be had from involving chastity in your life.

The allure of the sexy secret that only the two of you know about the control you have over him can be a big turn on, that can be used in your communication during the day
The fact that he is placing the woman's pleasure above his own doesn't mean that there is no love making. The teasing can be quite arousing and seeing his cock fill the device with his obvious feelings or arousal can be exciting in and of itself. Depending upon the device you may be able to slightly penetrate yourself with it which may give you great pleasure without reciprocating that pleasure to himself, the frustration of knowing and maybe even slightly feeling her pussy as she rubs it up and down the device will be an incredible turn on for him.

The tease could continue with her giving him oral sex, maybe touching what parts she can with the tip of her tongue or taking the device into her mouth. Make sure he is watching so he can see just what he is missing as you give him that blow job you promised him at dinner time, but he just didn't think it all the way through.

Foreplay is the thing now, and you should take full advantage of your lover spend as much time as you like kissing and touching and caressing, get out the feathers and oils and really do those things that you enjoy the most as you are in control.

If you are truly in the mood for penetration it doesn't have to be with his cock make him put the strapon belt on and he can fuck you with a much bigger cock without ever receiving any pleasure from it at all. They even make a device that his own cock slides into and hard or soft he won't feel a thing as he is giving you the fucking you always wanted and now with a cock that is touching you in places his little cock never could reach before.

When all is said and done you may ask should he be allowed to cum to orgasm and get his release. Yes he should but when and where that happens is up to you, and should never be the norm, if you don't want to make that decision the dice or a coin can take the place so he can't get upset about it.
Just keep reminding him how amazing that orgasm is going to be when he finally gets to have it.

It is always about the teasing and the romance and did I mention the teasing.

If you take the cock out of the experience you will find new and wonderful ways of being a part of each other's life, and he will strive to keep you satisfied in mind, body, and soul.

The Power

When a man gives up control of his cock, he is giving up the power of being a man. Now some will argue that a man is more than his sexual organ, and while that may be true, a man without a cock is not truly a man.

Now your woman or key holder, may become drunk with power, it certainly isn't unheard of, and as such you may find yourself in a far different place.

If you are one who can enjoy the darker side of fetish then here are some rules for those who are a little more adventurous and can handle more than the average person. For a woman who now holds your key may find herself free from her own bonds that society has placed upon her, and her growth and desires may require something more then what a submissive man can give her.

You will be locked up at all times that she does not have a use for your cock

( ) Yes
( ) He is not ready for this rule at this time
( ) No

You gave up the power and as such she will let you know when she wants your pathetic little cock to come out and play. It could very well be a long time before you get to touch the little guy again.

She however will enjoy the teasing and denial, playing games with you making your cock hard in its cage or case laughing at you as it pushes to be free but will not gain its freedom anytime soon.

You will pleasure me at any time, in any place, for however long I desire.
( ) Yes
( ) He is not ready for this rule at this time
( ) No

This one can start out real nice like honey come out on the porch and get down on your knees and lick me till I cum twice while I enjoy my coffee and watch the birds in our back yard. Which could quickly lead to, pull over in the rest area and get between my legs and make me cum, and I don't care if anyone is watching.

Now take out rest area and insert Beach or Poolside at the hotel.

What about at the restaurant where you are celebrating your Mother's birthday in the coat room.

Just imagine how exciting doing that in all those places will be though.

Your pathetic cock will be pushing at the bonds it finds itself in for certain.

Telling others
( ) Yes
( ) He is not ready for this rule at this time
( ) No

Well this could be a tough one, or it could be really fucking exciting too.

She may decide to do this behind your back so you won't even know but there is only a limited amount of fun in that.
How much better would it be if you were there when she fondles her key on her chain and turns to her friend and asks them if they know what this key is for?

Yup you are standing right there when she tells her best friend that she has you locked up in a chastity device. Of course the friend won't believe her which means you will be taking your pants down and probably your pretty panties if you are in this deep to show her best friend your pathetic cock encased in plastic or metal.

Of course she won't stop there soon she will tell the neighbors and then your own friends, everyone will know just what sort of man you really are or in this case aren't.

She will really have you by the balls then.

No Doctor, No Travel, No Gym, No Release
( ) Yes
( ) He is not ready for this rule at this time
( ) No

So it won't really matter if you are going to the Doctor unless the doctor needs to have access to your genitals so think how embarrassing it will be if you have to disrobe and have the nurse or your doctor see you in chastity.

If you are traveling I may or may not make you were a metal lock so you will go off through the metal detector and have to explain to the big masculine TSA agent why your crotch is causing his wand to make that noise, who knows maybe you will have to take a trip to the private room and show him you are in chastity.

Going to the gym or any other type of place will be humiliating as you have to change or disrobe and all the other real men will see your pathetic cock locked up and useless.

Butt plugs your new sex toy
( ) Yes
( ) He is not ready for this rule at this time
( ) No

Well since you can't touch yourself it is only fair that you have a toy you can play with and as such you only have one other place you can play with and that is your asshole.

You should be plugged for an ever increasing period of time during the day to be decided by your woman.

The plug will increase in size as you become accustomed to them.

Sex Change   (no not like that)
( ) Yes
( ) He is not ready for this rule at this time
( ) No

Sex is definitely going to change.

Your cock will remain locked up but you should still have a chance to orgasm or to at least cum, it is just not healthy to never get to cum again.

After I am fully satisfied sexually by either your tongue, your fingers or whatever toys I decide I want you to use on me. It will be your turn and no you will not be unlocked.

You will begin the process of learning what it feels like to be penetrated with a real cock.

During this time you will be allowed to freely ejaculate or orgasm as you see fit to with a big dick going in and out of your ass.

A plate or bowl will be placed under your locked up cock to catch what comes out, so that you can swallow it when we are done have your new special sex.

If you want to make the experience even more special you can moan and scream in a pretty girly voice since there is basically no man left in you other than the big rubber cock going into your ass.

After the first time if you are not already doing so you should start wearing panties afterwards since you don't deserve to even own men's underwear.

Something Big for me now
( ) Yes
( ) He is not ready for this rule at this time
( ) No

It isn't really fair that you get to have such a satisfying sexual experience.

So I think it is only fair that as the woman I get to find a big cock too.

I will have the right to start going out with the girls and leaving you locked up at home, maybe even tied to the bed until I get back.

I will have the right to request that you to find me a man with a large cock to satisfy me sexually.

If you fail to satisfy this request I will have the right to take matters into my own hands and find someone myself.

Clean Up Duties
( ) Yes
( ) He is not ready for this rule at this time
( ) No

If I do make you into a cuckold, you will be required to clean up any cum that any man has left on me or inside of me or anywhere else for that matter.

If the bull doesn't mind you will also clean his cock once he is done and you may even be required to fluff him for me getting him hard either the first time, second time, or tenth time as we see fit.

There may be times when I come home after a night out with the girls and require a good cleaning you will be tied to the bed during those nights out and upon my arrival home I will sit on your face so that you can clean out whatever cum may still be in whichever hole the gentlemen was allowed to cum in.

I may at times bring home condoms filled with the cum of the men that had sex that night, I may even request my girlfriends to give me their men's condoms as well so you can have an extra treat as I show you what a real man's cum looks like, or two, or three, or four.

Maybe it's time for a piercing
( ) Yes
( ) He is not ready for this rule at this time
( ) No

Adding a piercing and there are many places that a man's genitalia can be pierced, you can do temporary piercing or go for something more permanent.

You should always do your own research on things that are important and having your body pierced is a very important thing to think about, and even though the woman may be in charge any piercing must be voluntary and cannot be forced upon someone.

The Prince Albert is by far the most popular of piercings and surprisingly doesn't hurt anymore then getting your ears done even though it is probably one of the scariest to think about. There are some Chastity devices that can easily incorporate the Prince Albert into the method of being locked up.

The frenum is the underside of the penis, it doesn't go through the actual shaft of the penis.

Hafada/Scrotum – these are usually placed on the side of the sack but if you are using a chastity device you may run into issues unless you take placement into consideration with the device on.

Maybe it's time for a tattoo
( ) Yes
( ) He is not ready for this rule at this time
( ) No

Nothing says permanent like a tattoo, and like before on the piercing something of this nature needs to be consented by the party in question. You should certainly use your influence to make it something special.

Maybe it could be a pretty pink unicorn right above your crotch, or maybe a ball and chain or something else to indicate the current position of your chastity slave. So many things could indicate ownership a simple barcode right above his cock, is a nice an easy one.

Of course you could be more direct with some words like "Sissy" or "My Bitch", simply put "Slave".

Get creative but also agree on what it should be, it doesn't have to be on his crotch it could be anywhere you want it to be but it should be some representation of what you are doing it could be obvious or your little secret.

A Chastity Story

Here is a little story I wrote, I do so like writing little sissy cuckold locked up stories about men and their pathetic little cocks.

I hope you enjoy it.
~M.J.~

The moment I felt the cool liquid touch my skin and felt her fingers wrap around the shaft of my cock, I knew the session was over and I would be going back into the cage. The feelings of ecstasy still rolling up my spine, as well as the pangs of frustration knowing once again she was not going to let me have an orgasm.

"Not this time Henry, you know what I said earlier. You will be allowed to cum when that cock of yours shows some progress in getting smaller."

The ice cold liquid caused the back rush of blood away from the tip of my now softening penis.

"There, now that's better. See how much quicker it gets soft, very good Henry, that is a little progress isn't it?"
I nodded as the Mistress patted my back in encouragement.
"Now put yourself back together"

I watched her as she wiped her hands on the towel she now threw to the ground at my feet. Turning she made her way to the door of the room never looking back more concerned with her mobile phone and calling one of the lovers she had taken.

Glancing over I saw what putting myself together was made up of, the ring and the cage with the pegs and the of course the lock. The ring felt tight around my, what could only be described as my swollen balls. I say swollen, since Mistress has not allowed me to achieve an orgasm in almost two months now.

Once the ring was around both my balls and the now soft shaft of my cock, I had to admit they did have a slight color of blue. I tucked the shaft of my cock into the cage which in one click of a small padlock would encapsulate my cock with nothing more than a small slit to allow me to urinate through. I often left stains on my panties as I was often leaking pre-cum throughout the day.

Mistress encouraged my feminization; well probably demanded would be a more appropriate description. Aside from the panties, my body was kept hairless, which I had to admit I rather liked but was loath to tell her about. I found it hard to believe that I was enjoying aspects of the transformation that was occurring, well up until she began using that liquid on my cock, telling me that it was going to be a regular part of my routine that it would begin to shrink my penis. Evidently she felt that the smaller my cock was the more I would feel like a woman, or at least think less of wanting to play with it like a man.

I didn't believe her at first, but after the second application I noticed a tingling sensation, and before long I was having problems even getting an erection.

The tingling was in full tingle right now as I slid the pad lock through the hole in the chastity device. The panties I had been wearing were on the floor and I picked them up and slid them back up my legs, the slid easily because of the sheer thigh highs. They were crotch less-panties so the chastity device stuck through and was accessible, and yes they were pink.
I got up and left the room to find her. She was sitting by the bar talking to what sounded like Ricardo.

"Yes he can barely even get it up; I think I will see some better results in the next month or so."

She pointed to the ground and I knelt in front of her.

"Sure that would be great, I would love that, I know it makes me wet just thinking about it"

"Ok I will see you in a little bit then."

She laid the phone on the bar top and swiveling in the stool she sat in front of me with open legs.

"Stand Up"

I did this immediately, Mistress doesn't like to wait.

"I am glad you remembered, to put it through the hole for me."

Click...

It was done, nothing to do about it now she was once again in total control of its release.

The finger pointed down to the floor again.
I knelt.

"Seems I will be going out to Ricardo's house he has something to give me"

Her hand relaxed on my head tousling my hair.

"Now why don't you give a quick one with your tongue before I go."

She guided me between, knowing exactly where she wanted to have my tongue.

She always became wet when we had a session, the beatings she gave me were quite intensive, I really felt that she would one day actually orgasm from just causing me pain.

My tongue touched her outer lips, which were glistening and ran it up to flick her already swollen clit.

I began to work on her clit taking it into my mouth and wiggling my tongue back and forth and then up and down like I knew Mistress liked. It wasn't long before the pressure of her hands on my head increased, the scream that came next was filled with joy and pleasure and then her hands shook with a deep orgasm.

It a few moments for Mistress to pull herself together but when she was ready she dismissed me.

It was a good thing too for I was way behind on the daily chores, just because Mistress wants to play with me doesn't relieve me from doing all my chores.

Stepping into the grey plaid skirt which was just long enough to come to the tops of my thigh high stockings I felt like such a naughty schoolgirl when Mistress let me wear that one. The bra was a good quality that snapped in the front which made it easier for me to get into, followed by the white blouse and plaid tie. I was still in my black heels, didn't really have a choice as they had locks on them and I could only get out of them when Mistress let me. It took me a long time to get used to the heels; I had them on night and day for two weeks before I had mastered them.

I touched up the make up on my face and super high glossed my red lips, and then it was back to the laundry.

"I am going out Henry, please make sure the chores are finished else you will be sleeping on the floor tonight. Do you understand?"

"Yes Mistress"

"Good, if you are a good boy I will bring you home a treat, would you like that?"

"Yes Mistress"

I watched as she closed the door departing to Ricardo's house I knew she would be having sex with him, that was the only reason she went to Ricardo's home.

I didn't waste any time but got back to doing the laundry, I could hear the click as my padlock bounced around as I squatted in my heels to get access to the dryer.

After the laundry it was to the kitchen and the dishes and then the moping, the afternoon passed into early evening when I heard the door open. Mistress was arriving home, I immediately put down what I was doing so that I could greet her.

I quickly got to my knees, looking up at her beautiful face.

"Put your eyes to the floor, who do you think you are?"

"I am nothing Mistress"

"That is correct you are nothing, you are a pathetic excuse for what used to be a man"

"Ricardo was right I am just too soft on you"

"I have decided on a way to allow you to cum"

"Would you like that?"

"Oh yes Mistress, very much so"

"Well follow me"

Getting up from my knees I followed her to the back porch, she stepped out into the back yard and took out the necklace that held the key to my chastity belt, it was in fact the only key to my chastity belt as she had purposely bent and broke the spare key to show how important it was.

The key slid off the chain easily and fell to the palm of her hand.

"So here is how it will work"

I watched as she reached back and threw the key out into the yard somewhere, I was facing her so I couldn't see wear it went.

"When all of your chores are done and I have nothing for you to do, you can go out and look for the key, when you find it I will allow you to cum, and then throw it out there again."

"See now isn't that fair"

"Yes Mistress"

In reality I didn't think it was fair at all since my daily chores took me almost all day to do and then it would be hard to find in the dark, and we had a big back yard.

"Good, now why don't you get back on your knees and you can have your treat now."

"Seems Ricardo had a few friends over and, well let us just say they supersized your treat today"

I looked at her well fucked pussy and knew the cum was deep inside and as I began to lick the cum up that was just loosely stuck to her crotch I could taste the salty creamy liquid mixed with her own. My tongue delved into her opening and I was further rewarded with quite a bit in one shot. It was so erotic swallow cum from the men who had just fucked her, knowing my own load was building and building. I was sure I was already leaking into my panties leaving a wet spot.

I would have to finish up my chores quickly when I was done cleaning her so I could spend some time in my new favorite place the backyard, looking for my key so I could be allowed to release my own load while my cock was still large enough to do so.

In Conclusion

So let us review a few things as we come to a conclusion.
This book is purely for entertainment purposes and is not a
guideline on how to live your life.
With that said.

Don't do stupid things; utilizing chastity in a healthy
adventurous sexual relationship can bring you some amazing
feelings and emotions on both sides of the device.

As with anything it is important to have a very open and
truthful discussion about things before hand and though it
can be fun to push someone's boundaries people can often get
hurt if things are taken to far in the wrong direction.
Always be safe about the use of any toy, beware of sharp
edges or inappropriate constriction of blood vessels. Blue
balls are all fun and good but if your testicles die because of it,
not so much fun anymore.

Be responsible partners to each other.

Don't do things you can't take back.

Tying your partner to a chair so he can watch you have sex
with a stranger without both of you agreeing to cuckolding
can have serious repercussions on your relationship.

Apply common sense generously.

Having all the power doesn't mean you can do whatever you want. Giving up all the power doesn't mean you don't have any responsibility for what goes one.

So girls lock him up, tease him relentlessly, watch his cock strain against the device, let him cool down and then tease him again over and over until his pre-cum is dripping from the end.

Get him on his knees with his face between your legs licking your pussy and kissing your ass, until you explode with multiple orgasms.

Send him to bed frustrated as often as you can, he will be much more pliable when he hasn't came in a few days. Make a list of chores for him to do, have him impress you with his cooking and cleaning. Teach him to iron and fold your panties. Hell for that matter get him in panties and stockings, penetrate him let him find out what a little Anal feels like.

Do whatever makes you both happy and satisfied.

A Note from the Author

Well here it is the end of another project, I get mixed feelings when I come to the end of a project, I enjoy writing so much that I am sad to be at the end but at the same time I know that now others will get a chance to experience my wonderful lustful and sometimes sadistic thoughts. I just have so much fun writing about the experiences I have with my own submissive play things, they are such good little boi's all dressed so pretty and they do whatever I ask of them, well they know they will be punished if they don't.

So now it is your turn to once again do what I ask of you. I would like to hear from you, I am going to give you my personal email address so you can contact me so that I can get your feedback on the stories and the assignments and anything else you would like to tell me about. I would love to hear about your own stories and experiences, I just love it when I get email from the people who read my work, so don't hesitate to contact me, who knows maybe I will give you a special assignment just for you.

Write to me soon........I always write back....

Love

Mistress Jessica

Mistressjessica01@gmail.com

www.ingramcontent.com/pod-product-compliance
Lightning Source LLC
Chambersburg PA
CBHW060217290526
45789CB00003B/1301